Dysfunction:

Identify it. Discover the truth you've been hiding from yourself, probably most of your life.

Own it. Admit your part in the problems that are holding you back from your goals.

Eliminate it. Free yourself from your self-destructive past with innovative techniques that will change your life.

KUDOS for *Dysfunction:*
Identify It, Own It, Eliminate It

"Finally, hands-on experience for the rest of us." – *Brandi Hitt, Anchor, ABC News*

"Dysfunction is a short but powerful book that I believe every one of us needs to read at least once. Whether or not you come from a dysfunction family or are part of a dysfunctional relationship, you undoubtedly know someone who does or is. The great thing about this book is that it tells you how to fix the problems in yourself, but it also gives you some insight so you have a better understanding of how to deal with the problem in others." – *Taylor, Reviewer*

"I enjoyed the case studies he presented and thought it was an excellent way to make his points. I personally found the information to be extremely helpful and informative. Sort of like a "Dysfunctional Personalities for Dummies" book. It's a handy little guide to dysfunctional hang-ups in yourself or others. It gives a good explanation of what the problems are, how to recognize them in yourself and others, and how to deal with them." – *Regan, Reviewer*

ACKNOWLEDGEMENTS

My best teachers over the years have had quirky traits. For example, the psychiatric social worker who had to have her pencils aligned in parallel on the desk during our supervision sessions. Another was the internationally acclaimed psychoanalytic theorist and classic pianist who still bit his nails. You might say they initiated me into the world of dysfunction. I learned to see it in my clients and recognize it in the therapists. They served to legitimize the development of an honest self-analysis that each day facilitates my work with others. I owe them, and a host of other teachers, a mountain of gratitude for all they taught me.

"The teacher appears when the student is ready."

This book is about becoming ready and accepting the task of learning about yourself. My ability to convey these ideas has been made possible only through my participation in a writing critique group led by Bonnie Hearn Hill. The Tuesdays represented a large number of published authors who met for several years with Bonnie at the helm. The Fridays group started as the Tuesdays wound down, and it continues to meet weekly. I have been fortunate to be part of the Fridays for the last several years.

The first time I met Bonnie, I knew that I had found my new teacher. She seemed clairvoyant. She was able to predict the start of my novel without reading a page. She understood that much about writing. Over the years, her incisive comments made me want to write more. She didn't only help me focus my writing; she served as an example of a writer who strives to reach the next level. Her skill in leading me to find my voice has challenged me to grow as a person and a writer.

Hazel Dixon-Cooper reminded me that astrology and psychology have common roots in the ageless wisdom that is communicated through story and mythology. We both share a passion for looking below surface appearances to understand human nature. She has taught me that our theoretical perspectives are not so different, and that the goal of both frameworks is to communicate to the client in a way that enables them to make practical changes.

Christopher Allan Poe is an established musician and author. He combined hard work along with his natural ability to reveal a broad scope of talent. He has both critiqued my writing and consulted on the art work. He is brilliant and generous.

Other members of the Fridays and Tuesdays writing groups have continued to be supportive over the years, and always offered criticism that helped me hone my message.

My wife and three daughters have brought humor and joy to life. They have sacrificed family time to enable me to pursue my writing. In addition, they always brought a fresh point of view as naive readers when I would finally let them read my work.

My editor Lauri Wellington had the vision to understand the concept of dysfunction, and the skill to edit the manuscript to uncover its strengths. She contributed to the clarity of the overall work by identifying those concepts that required elaboration. She helped my voice be more authentic and clear.

My patients, whose names must remain confidential, teach me each day to recognize the reality of their pain. They have demonstrated that the only way through heartache is to identify the problem, face it, and develop a new relationship to it. Identify it. Own it. Eliminate it.

To, all of you, a heartfelt thank you.

DYSFUNCTION:

IDENTIFY IT. OWN IT.
ELIMINATE IT.

by

Dennis C. Lewis, Ph.D.

A BLACK OPAL BOOKS
PUBLICATION

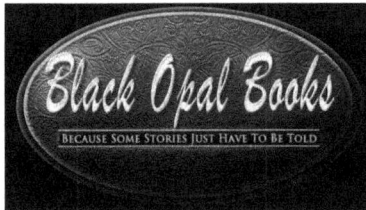

GENRE: NON-FICTION/SELF-HELP

This book is a work of non-fiction. All information and opinions expressed herein are the views of the author. This publication is intended to provide accurate and authoritative information concerning the subject matter covered and is for informational purposes only. Neither the author nor the publisher is attempting to provide legal advice of any kind or to diagnose any medical condition.

To my patients
who have had the courage to change and the
willingness to let me accompany them on the journey

TABLE OF CONTENTS

INTRODUCTION

First Steps to Healing
"Do or do not. There is no try." – Yoda

Though his book is about dysfunction. More important, it is about healing. If you're a member of the human race, you've probably been involved in a dysfunctional relationship or two. Welcome to the club. The nature of dysfunction produces a repetitive behavior pattern, and if you don't own it and eliminate it, you will end up repeating history. The majority of people have.

You know that if you have a broken leg, you have to get it fixed. Otherwise, it won't heal properly. You might still be able to walk, but you'll have a limp or an uneven gait, along with the possibility of injuring other parts of your body. The same applies to your emotional life. If you don't change dysfunctional behavior, you impede your ability to reach your goals and feel comfortable with yourself. Your problems will continue into the future and will affect your choices, your relationships, and your health.

Healing requires that you face what's wrong in order to change it. You can no longer ignore the emptiness in your life. Each day that you pretend everything is fine, you prevent the healing from starting. Perhaps you're afraid to admit to anyone how much trouble you are having keeping up appearances. You dread being exposed.

Emotional healing happens every day. It is marked by growth and development as you live your life. Healing requires you to identify a unifying theme within yourself that anchors you and gives you purpose. You are meant to become a fully functional person. Dysfunction is only a temporary stop on the path to healing. You don't need to stay there. You can move on.

Dysfunction affects everyone. The trap you feel holding you back could be due to childhood abuse, trauma, or neglect. Your parent might have been absent or smothering. You may have experienced unavoidable trauma. Deciding who's responsible only leads you closer to righteous indignation, which cements your identity as a victim. Assigning blame doesn't help you heal. Your way out is in the other direction.

The goal of this book is to help you identify the hole in your life that prevents you from moving forward.

CHAPTER 1

DYSFUNCTION AND SHAME

Avoid the Pitfalls

Patients often enter therapy saying that they know what their problem is. Many times they do. But they get stuck at that point and don't change because they haven't owned the dysfunction. Whether or not you can describe your conflicts better than a university professor doesn't count. You can't make changes by discussing the problem at arm's length. That's what I mean by owning it. You can't change anything you don't claim as your own.

Fear of encountering the negative keeps many patients from moving forward. Jung spoke about it as avoidance of the shadow element in the personality. Instead of protecting them from being contaminated by the negative, the one-sided focus prevents growth. Pop psychology emphasizes adopting a positive attitude, and it has an impressive track record. However, the patient's understanding is translated more often into superficial affirmations that preserve the status quo. You could call it the fear of change. It keeps the patient cemented to what is familiar in an effort to ward off anxiety.

The dysfunctional family could be considered a defender of propriety, the upholder of arbitrary beliefs that allow its members to believe the world is predictable and fixed. This wish produces a rigidity in thinking that limits options rather than facilitating growth. The excessive need for security leads to the fear of change and pushes a patient further into dysfunctional solutions.

Encountering Unavoidable Obstacles:

When people hit an impasse and the old solutions don't work, they are forced to look for a new way of addressing the problem. I talk to my patients about this experience as "hitting the wall." Everyone does at some point in life. We might be 45 when we hit our wall. Or 65, or 85, or even 25. It doesn't matter whether memories from past trauma surface, or an incurable disease strikes. When we hit the wall we have to look for new tools to address the current crisis. The best option is looking at the problem head on.

To do this, a person must confront the emotional hook that keeps him or her attached to his or her family and to the pathology of making excuses. Anyone raised in a dysfunctional family recoils from the challenge of growth. Nothing is more frightening than the vulnerability of change. However, we cannot shrink from taking action out of fear that it will hurt too much to remove the hook. The temptation is to resolve to change without ditching the habits of yesterday. The familiar, even if painful, is tolerable. The unknown is not.

The dysfunctional family member fears abandonment and emptiness. In order to avoid being overwhelmed with these emotions, he or she holds onto the old habits for dear life. You can feel safe this way but never truly satisfied or independent. If this applies to you, your task is to recognize the sequence for what it is, and address the fear at the first opportunity.

Keeping Up Appearances:

In the dysfunctional family, a false front becomes the public representation held out to the world. You might hide behind this screen knowing that it is not real. The resulting distortion of the truth controls not only the external display but also your internal experience.

Total denial, which blocks awareness of the truth, last only a short time. When that fails, alternate explanations arise that cannot withstand the weight of fact. Your sense of self falters, and fear forces a further change in awareness. This is called disassociation. Whereas denial blocks the truth, dissociation alters your connection to yourself. It is a form of self-alienation.

∾∾

Case Study: Barbara:

Barbara always told everyone that her daddy was not around the house on weekends because he was a doctor. Actually, he was a dentist, and he spent the weekends with his girlfriend. Her own misconstruction presented a living fiction that she began believing herself. As she did, her grasp on reality started slipping away. She used denial first, which replaced "what is" with "what is believed." When that didn't work, she retreated from the conflict by dissociating. Dissociation alienates you from yourself and dulls your awareness in the face of threat, perceived or real. Denial combined with dissociation resulted in Barbara being detached, or more significantly, absent in relationships. She resided in a fantasy that didn't challenge her to exist on a feeling level. She could remain lost to the present and reside in the story of her own liking. After all, her father hadn't abandoned the family but live a life in service to others.

Barbara was what we call a *pretender*. They behave as if everything is all right with the world. Using the term pretender to describe the person trapped in the dysfunctional family is less pathological and acknowledges the temporary nature of the adjustment. In order to grow, you have to stop pretending and begin living in the moment in a more authentic way.

Keeping up appearances is not unique to pretenders, but how they use it differentiates them from *normals*. Both project a certain image to bolster self-esteem. The difference is that pretenders rely on a falsehood and are conflicted about it at the same time. Normals hold socially acceptable beliefs that enable them to cope with the risks encountered in everyday life. A common example is, "It will never happen to me." That sentiment allows them to minimize the reaction to stress and to preclude a constant state of crisis.

The other behavior that distinguishes normals from pretenders is that when memories of unhappy moments in their history surface, they can hold that experience in mind and have the associated feeling. For instance, if you ask a normal about losing a parent, she might tear up as she tells you about how terrible Mom's last days in the hospital were. Pretenders will avoid showing any feeling, but they will tell you how good the nurses were.

Many normals share similar challenges or trauma that pretenders have growing up. When stressed, everyone tries to preserve their self-esteem. The difference between a normal and a pretender lies in whether the solution you choose requires a temporary shift (normal) in your self-concept or a more permanent one (pretender). When your response fits within your concept of self, you become functional or normal. If you have to resort to distorting your self-concept in order to cope, you survive but with a loss of ego integrity. Chain a number of these types of events together, and you diverge from the norm into dysfunction.

Literature offers crystallized examples of these two outcomes. For instance, Harry Potter and Tom Riddle (also known as Lord Voldemort) were both orphans. Harry grew up in the less than perfect home of his aunt and uncle. Riddle dominated other children at the orphanage and developed a cruel nature. They both reached stable adjustments, but one led to integration of the person and the second to disintegration.

Family Influence:

Dysfunction exists within family relationships and interactions. The choices that you make, the relationships you have, and the responses you receive from significant others are interwoven as strands running through the same fabric. When an event occurs during your developmental years that impacts your self-esteem, as in Barbara's case, a primitive injury becomes part of the family story. It might be the loss of a parent or other traumatic experience. When the theme is embedded in the family narrative of either the adult or the child, everyone feels the pull. That's all you might be aware of because family secrets are often hidden or minimized. Still, the reverberations from key events will affect you. The depression, drug use, or anxiety in your parents can create a divot for you growing up. You're already starting with one foot in the gutter.

Shame and the False Front:

If the false front is the face of the family, denial is the individual framing. Together they block the sharp edge of shame that threatens the pretenders of the family. The negative message carried in the dysfunctional family is not only that you are wrong, but also unworthy. The false front colludes with denial in shielding you from self-incrimination. In this situation, innocence fills you and allows you to believe that all is fine with the world. The pretense goes on.

Denial and the false front construct a shiny dome over the dysfunctional family with the unique characteristic of repelling the abhorrent and allowing the warmth of the sun to both penetrate and reflect off of it. The family continues to polish the surface, keeping the protective barrier in place while beginning to see themselves in the distorted reflection.

The Dome Experience:

Family members often get trapped in this compulsive pattern of *polishing the dome*. From the outside, everything looks perfect. The pretender commits to maintaining an image, a transparent covering that shields the family name by preserving the façade of the false front. This feel-good fantasy has a dual purpose. The first is to protect the status quo. The pretender can see him or herself in the polished surface, and the reflection confirms that everything is okay. But the nagging hint that something is not quite right persists and can threaten the illusion. At such times, he or she climbs under the dome, content to hunker down with the familiar. Inside the dome, the false front stands secure, protected from weather, insult, and most of all, inspection.

What does your family dome look like? A sign that you're activating the dome experience is when you find yourself defending your parents or family to others. How often have you caught yourself saying, "That's just Dad." Or, "that's only his second 'driving under the influence.'"

Temporarily during this activity, your reflection in the shiny dome looks good. When you climb under the dome, you can feel confident in its protection. For the dysfunctional family, the dome becomes a prison. The only consolation is you are all together.

❧❧❧

Case Study, Sharon:

Sharon, married to an alcoholic for thirty years, lived under the dome. She attended Al-Anon faithfully. Still, she held onto the fantasy that Bob was sober, that they were happily married, and that he just relapsed at times. After an early evening school performance that our children were in, I noticed that he was drunk, and asked her, "What's with Bob?"

She tilted her head as she looked across the gymnasium. He stood with another group of parents, waving his hands wildly and talking loudly. I had initiated the conversation with Sharon but abided by the unwritten rule of not actually talking about the problem drinking.

She looked back to me. "What good will it do to confront him?" She wanted an assurance of a positive benefit of exposing her feelings.

"He has to know it affects you," I said.

She feared being contaminated by her own negative emotions. "You tell him."

They were friends, so I did what I wouldn't have ventured to do if she had been a patient. I followed Bob when he went out to the parking lot to smoke.

"Hey, that was some performance, wasn't it?"

He laughed. "This artsy-fartsy stuff doesn't teach these grade-schoolers anything, and you know that." His eyes were bloodshot, and his voice was slurred.

"I was just talking with Sharon." I paused hoping that time would let that sink in. "It's hard to appreciate anything when you've been drinking."

"Is that what she told you?"

"I'm concerned for you. If you ever want to chat about it."

"Sharon and I are fine," he said. "She has no problem with me." He crushed out his cigarette and went back into the auditorium.

When I entered, I couldn't find him or Sharon. That was the last time I spoke to either of them. He resented the intrusion. She pretended to change by attending meetings and holding onto the old familiar agreement with Bob.

ოოო

Have you ever been stuck like that? Afraid that you might feel too much? When you cut yourself off from the negative feelings, you block emotion in general, except for the pretend feelings. They thrive under the dome in stereotypic *word packages. We had a wonderful Christmas! So good to see you.* These social conventions harm you by blocking your access to your real feelings. They serve as emotional insulation as if your real feelings were flammable.

Confronting your feelings is the first step toward healing. There is no other way.

ece

Case Study, Sally:

In group therapy sessions, Sally dominated the discussion for four sessions with the repetitive story of the abuse she suffered growing up. She said she was very angry. But during the fifth meeting, she actually felt the anger and could begin to acknowledge it to herself in a new way. This was the first time she had cried in more than fifteen years. She managed to crack the family dome.

ece

Most pretenders need a guide to help them navigate from behind the false front and out from under the dome. To fight your way free the first time is a monumental struggle, but you can do it. Remembering to come out each morning to face your fears requires courage.

Confronting the False Front:

The immediate focus is for you to avoid accepting the complacency of early changes as a final solution. Dysfunctional families create a distorted view of the world that swallows new behaviors and spreads them across the dome. The surface shines brighter because you attempted to change. The message to you is that just an attempt is enough. Don't be fooled.

Real people have feelings that are not toxic or life threatening. When crisis follows crisis, you begin to believe that the whole world functions as if on the brink of collapse. That's not true. You might have lived according to the saying, "When you have only a hammer, every problem is a nail." Your feelings are more complicated than that, and if you are honest enough to look at them, you can grow.

You can escape the definitions given you at birth. Freud was right. Research on early attachment has shown that much of our personality is established by age five. The good news is that if you stop pretending, you don't always have to act like a four-year-old.

Dysfunctional dependency is acted out and resolved within relationships with family and friends. Re-examine these. Do you focus on others and end up cut off from yourself? If so, talk to those who are important to you and risk letting them know who you are. Do the work now and you may save your life.

To do this, you will have to overcome your resistance. The barriers to growth are walls of fear that block progress, but as you begin to recognize your fears, you can face them and gain a new perspective from the top.

It may be difficult to envision now, but you can develop a different connection to your family and others that enables you to be a whole person. The closest analogy is that of empowerment, when you stand comfortably by yourself and yet are aware of your role in the relationship.

Practice independence within day-to-day tasks. Ask yourself whether what you are doing is consistent with your goals and desires. Sure, washing dishes is no one's favorite pastime. Everyday chores like preparing meals are part of life. But ask yourself if your spotless home is purchased at the expense of your growth? Find time to devote to your goals.

You know that living more fully is possible. If you're ready to examine how your family has imprisoned you in a distorted, limiting view of yourself, then read on. Remember that legacy is not measured by the glamour or sheen of the family crest, but carried within the pain and struggle that you have already lived. Resolving the trauma rather than just setting it behind you will lead to richness you would otherwise not know.

Next, you'll see that what you tell yourself changes your understanding of life, and more important, how you experience it.

CHAPTER 2

MIND MESSAGES

Revise the Negative Script

Maintaining the false front requires that you tell yourself lies every day. Little white lies make life more bearable for others. You say to your friend, "I'm sure he didn't mean that," to help her feel better after an insult. When you're criticized, you tell yourself, "She's just jealous."

These explanations preserve your self-esteem and prevent you from being overwhelmed by emotions. However, if you rely on such temporary solutions too often, you develop an external shell that cuts you off from experiencing life. Never mind that the cardboard smile you show to the outer world belies the fear you feel in your heart. The ideal you hold in your head about how the world is supposed to be is a flimsy replica of real life sustained by a lie. While perpetuating the lie, you lose touch with your deeper nature. The accompanying dishonesty contributes to the dysfunction in the family.

Remember that dysfunctional habits can be changed. You can learn how to stop lying to yourself. You can stop pretending and live your life for real. In order to grow, you have to identify and confront your earliest fears. By doing so, you encounter what psychologist Henry Murray called the *Unity Thema*, the core set of needs that determines your life course.

Primitive Life Scripts:

Your identity is anchored in your personal story. Nature has established specific biological factors such as your hair color and height. Within the narrative, however, is a story that you are responsible for creating. You, as the main character, drive the action and make the decisions. The problem is that you will do nearly anything to enhance your self-image. The little white lies that sneak in first as window dressing end up as the main buttress for preserving your self-esteem. The phony front you hold onto as your persona, a term Jung used, risks the loss of self similar to the studio lot façade that falls for lack of supports. In my experience, these self-preservation lies for most people cluster around a few basic stories.

The scenes from the *Happy Childhood* fantasy allow you to feel as if you lived with the Cleavers. Many clients offer this picture as a synopsis of their developmental years. When I probe, the details reveal a completely different story. For example, Crystal's story romanticized a nomadic existence as the family followed Dad in search of work. International locations were supposed to enrich her education. Instead, the main lesson she learned was that no friendship is permanent. Trusting others didn't come naturally for her. She subjected even close friends to tests and found them unreliable. She fled three marriages and blamed the husband each time.

Another common theme is the *Dependable Child Syndrome*. In reality this is better called the *orphan*. Not a child whose parents have died, but one who has had responsibility forced upon him or her too early. Carol recounted how she went home from school each day, let herself into the house, started her homework, and cooked dinner. She was proud of her independence and maturity. In therapy for depression twenty years later, she had trouble accepting that the seven-year-old latch key kid never grew up. From seven to seventeen, she held onto a pseudo maturity while remaining a little girl on the inside. Proper, conventional responses covered for a profound emptiness. Conformity for its own sake became a principle she expected, or rather demanded, of herself and others.

The Free Spirit pretends that spontaneous self-expression is the only road to creativity. Conventional living supposedly represents a surrender of one's individuality.

❧❧❧

Case Study, Luke:

As a free spirit, Luke felt justified in devoting his time and energy to his music. When he left his wife with two young children, he explained that he had to be an example to them of what it meant to pursue your dream. His friend offered him a room at the time of the separation believing only the harshest of circumstances could have led him to abandon his children. After six months of sponging off the friend, Luke switched to working on his novel. "Creativity can't be bridled," he said.

❧❧❧

The Perfectionist can't handle anger. In order to disguise the possible explosions, he or she camouflages them within a rubric of order and discipline.

❧❧❧

<u>Case Study, Peter</u>:

Peter said he appreciated that his buzz-cut Marine dad had taught him a strong work ethic. From age six, his bed had to be made before breakfast, and the drill-sergeant-of-a-dad made the morning inspection. He had to please his dad and thought that giving 100 percent was the only way to be adequate. Later in his life, he disciplined his wife for improperly prepared meals. His actions resulted in frequent visits from the sheriff for domestic violence calls. His feelings of failure, however, came from not achieving the ideal.

えかんる

Changing the Self-Concept:

Can you see yourself in one of these core types? My patients come to therapy with a tenaciously held belief about who they are. Whether they can state what their core issue is or not, the changes are still difficult. For instance, maybe you have left the perfectionist behind you only to discover that the myth of the happy childhood couldn't bear the full weight of your emotional distress. Maybe you continue to lie to yourself in order to bolster your self-esteem rather than confront the core issue that haunts you. When you can face what you're afraid of in yourself, you can make changes.

Parental Admonitions:

Many of the familiar lies that support normal behavior arise out of the admonitions that you stored up from childhood. They represent an interconnected network of thoughts that are tied to early experiences. Here are the top ten parental admonitions of all time:

1. You should know better.
2. Bad boy.
3. Don't feel. Don't think. Don't tell.
4. Because I said so.
5. Be a good girl.
6. If you don't have anything nice to say, don't say anything at all.
7. Shame on you.
8. Just suck it up.
9. No one loves a whiner.
10. I'll give you something to cry about.

Each one of these asks you to deny part of your own experience and commit to preserving the family lie. After all, if you confront the myth of the happy childhood, the implications can affect the family, maybe the extended family, or even the entire neighborhood.

Any single admonition can be applied in various situations, and has a certain utility. Each statement instructs you how to respond, rather than teaching you how to assess, evaluate, and decide. You basically forfeit any sense of self-determination.

The parental statements accuse you of behaving badly or making an error. However they go further. Each one, in some way, invokes a sense of shame. The underlying message that your unconscious hears loud and clear, doesn't say that you have made a mistake that will need to be fixed. Rather, it says that you *are* the mistake that can't be fixed.

A Remedy:

The next time you feel down on yourself, see if you can hear the parental admonition that is lurking in the recesses of your mind. Glance at the above list to help uncover at least the tone of the parental voice. Identify the childhood script that helps carry the feeling.

Next, ask yourself what you are trying to protect. A frequent answer is, "Mom did the best she could." Depending upon your circumstance, that sentence can be finished with, "with all the children she had." Or, "considering she was hooked on crack." Or, "with the upbringing she had." All excuses. All part of the lie in your life. You don't have to protect anyone any more. You are only responsible for your own decisions.

When you have walked through these steps, you will experience a sense of relief and lightness that will enable you to address the next challenge with truth. First, reflect on your life story and identify the themes that you see.

Second, ask yourself if there is a distortion in your story that tries to cover up the truth. For example, Richard came from such a close-knit family, each of the siblings had to move three thousand miles away from each other.

Third, see if you recall a statement that your parents repeated to you that stands out in your mind. If so, that statement likely has deep roots and affects how you think and live your emotional life.

Last, take responsibility for your feelings, and identify your own direction. Each day, pause for a moment and take a deep breath. Close your eyes and see if you can center yourself in your environment. Relax. Then open your eyes and look for any elephant standing in the room.

Once you identify your negative script, you're ready to see the broader themes acted out over the ages in mythology. Welcome to the historic stage. Recognize yourself?

CHAPTER 3

STUCK ON REPLAY

Expose Your Personal Myth

You have seen how your story might mirror general themes and that parental input can have a profound effect on your reactions. These occur at the conscious level; however, timeless patterns from mythology resonate to bring forth stories from your unconscious. While the grand story of your family is not on the scale of the *Odyssey*, recognizing the myth informs you of the set-up, the pitfalls, and the possible solutions. By identifying the character you play in your family's history, you can gain perspective. Your task is similar to the main character in any saga. You must overcome an obstacle and, in so doing, learn about yourself.

☙❧☙

Case Study, John:

John suffered under the legacy of the family estate that controlled a farming enterprise in Central California. The family name was known in every household. He expressed concern about protecting his confidentiality. He needed to pay the bill in cash, he insisted, so there were no bank records. He was a giant of agriculture.

The myth became destructive when it required him to act out a personal lie. John paid cash to hide his identity not due to his stature but due to his feelings of insignificance. His older brother managed the farm. The other brother controlled all the finances. John managed some apartments in town. He already occupied the lowest rung on the family ladder. No one could know he needed help.

Every family myth contains some secret that the family prefers to ignore. John's was no different. His family's philanthropy was built on the wealth accumulated during the confinement of Japanese farmers in World War II. The patriarch was considered by some to be an opportunist, by others to be a thief. Either way, the apartment-managing grandson was ashamed and depressed. Treatment couldn't start until he exposed the family history.

♥♥♥

Your family myth might not be so dramatic. But it is operative anyway. You don't have to be educated in classic literature in order to apply this approach to your situation. You only have to stand back and see the full scope of your family story.

Self-Centeredness—the Story of Narcissus:

The handsome Greek hunter angered the gods and was cursed to fall in love with his own reflection. He pined away at the bank of the river, staring into the water. His story is the origin of the English word *narcissist*.

Numerous variations on this theme show up in therapy. This character type, either man or woman, sees none of his or her faults and cannot develop reciprocity in relationships. In marriage, he seeks adulation. But like Narcissus, he never gets enough.

♥♥♥

Case Study, Scott:

Scott never encountered troubles growing up. His mother rebuffed any penalties for his behavior—from kicking mud on the girls at kindergarten recess, to selling pot before high school graduation. She blamed anyone else for the actual problem. He suffered no consequences for anything. As an adult, he recruited others to provide unconditional approval similar to his mother's. He hit the wall after fifteen years of marriage. His wife's request for a divorce was the first real message he let sink in. True to form, he felt devastated for the few seconds it took him to decide that she never really loved him.

ოოო

What Was Your Family's Story?:

Case Study, June:

June, a free-lance journalist, came to therapy only after admitting that she couldn't work. Her husband confronted her when she hadn't budged from the couch for more than a week. Her regular physician told her that she had reached the maximum dose for the antidepressant she was taking. In her first session, she looked hopeless. Her sallow complexion and lack of make-up provided little contrast to her shoulder-length, pale brown hair. She talked about how her childhood was filled with good memories. Her mother had elected to stay home before returning to teaching when June was in junior high. During her session two weeks later, she complained about how she hated going to the sitter's.

The scene in my mind's eye changed from her mother being at home to June returning to an empty house. "I thought you told me that your mom didn't start work until you entered seventh grade," I said.

She smiled. "No. I went to a neighbor lady who watched me all through grade school."

My image of her life shifted. "When did you start that?"

She stared past me into the garden outside the window. She looked back to me and said, "I think it might have started before kindergarten. What does it matter? I don't remember."

"What is your earliest memory?"

"Being dropped off at the babysitter's." She shrugged. "I was always there when my sister went to her dance classes."

In subsequent sessions, she had no awareness that she alternated between blaming her parents and defending them. Her mother favored the older sister and bragged to relatives that she was so much smarter than June. Even so, June contended that Mom had no faults.

She blocked out that her mother had basically abandoned her to the sitter. June could tell me that her sister was the favorite but could not let that rejection really sink in. The early loss exerted a depressive tug on her from the shadows. She wished for a relationship in the present that would redeem the past. Lacking it, she kept pursuing the connection that had never been there.

During her career, she sent her mother a copy of each of her articles accepted for publication. Her mother never responded.

֎֍֎

Case Study, Camille:

No one knew why Camille did poorly in school, used drugs, and repeatedly cut her wrists. The adolescent treatment program recommended brief hospitalizations and required a "no self-harm" contract. Her parents couldn't keep her in therapy. She contacted me after she turned eighteen and could pursue therapy on her own terms.

It took five sessions before she revealed that her grandfather had molested her from age 5 to 11. Given her age, she was in control of whether the crime got reported to authorities. She broke the family secret in my office and had expected instant relief of the burden. When that didn't occur, she realized that she had to do more in order to heal. The first step required her to share the story with her mother and sisters.

She deliberately chose Easter to make her disclosure. All of her sisters would be gathered at Mom's house to fix dinner. The men traditionally stayed out of the kitchen during the holiday preparation.

"I wanted you all to know that when I was little, Grandpa used to come into my room at night," she said.

Her oldest sister looked at her across the kitchen. "So?"

No one else seemed to hear at first.

"It was in the middle of the night. He didn't come in to read me a bedtime story. He touched me."

Her sister shrugged. "That was just the way Grandpa was."

"What do you mean?"

Another sister deposited the carrots in the sink. "He always told me I was his favorite, but I didn't believe him."

Camille felt like she had been punched in the stomach. She laid down the knife fearing that she might faint. "It happened to all of you?"

Her four sisters nodded.

"It wasn't like he hurt us or anything," another sister said.

"Well, he hurt me," she said. "How could you know this and not protect me?"

She heard sobbing in the corner where her mother sat peeling apples. "I asked him to stop. He promised he would. I'm so sorry." Her mother ran from the room.

Her oldest sister turned on her. "Now see what you've done. You've upset Mom. Why'd you bring this up anyway?"

Camille learned that her mother had been his first victim, that her sisters had suffered silently before her, and that no one had reached out to protect her. In her rage, she found herself standing alone, alienated from family, but owning her own voice.

Numerous Greek tragedies involve incest and usually result in calamity. Camille's courage to speak out bought her a lesson that carried not only additional pain, but also the potential for healing. She stood back and saw her experience in broader perspective. She abandoned the line that "Mom did the best she could."

She understood Mom as victim and wanted to neither fault her nor excuse her. Camille had to stand with her own feelings and be responsible for those in the present. She stopped slashing her wrists.

ഗ৵ഗ

The Trickster Who Deceives Himself—Sisyphus and the Rock:

Sisyphus tricked everyone, even the gods. The best-known part of his story involves Sisyphus having the tables turned. To atone for his misdeeds, he was to roll a boulder to the top of a hill. When he completed the task,

Sisyphus would be freed of any further duty to the gods. However, his additional curse was that as he reached the top, the stone slipped and rolled down to the base of the mountain.

☙❧☙

Case Study, Jim:

Jim, the son of two alcoholic parents, shared the curse of Sisyphus. He had to repetitively solve his problem. In one session with me, he bravely confronted his own fears, set forth a plan to address relationship issues in his marriage, and left the session with the resolve to take action. The next session, the boulder rested at the base of the mountain again. He had negated his plan. He acted at first as if we hadn't talked about it, but then feigned chagrin that no doubt covered his shame. I wasn't disappointed as his therapist. He had resorted to pretending. In order to avoid feeling distressed, he blocked out any recall of his failure to complete his therapy assignment.

The deceit in this situation involves a process of self-alienation described as dissociation. In the extreme case, the individual assumes a separate identity, as in multiple personality disorder. In the more usual presentation, it involves a compartmentalization of emotional memory.

In the office, he demonstrated what occurred routinely at home. Jim had to split off the realization that his wife's nagging replicated the abuse he received when his parents were drunk. The marriage coasted on the smooth period between clashes. He would never resolve the relationship issues without addressing the reverberation of the family pathology. What needed to be uncovered from the *compartment of emotional forgets* was his parents' cycle of drinking, sobering up, swearing off, and diving in again.

eɔeɔ

Love at Any Cost—Cupid and Psyche

Psyche was a beautiful woman cursed by a jealous deity to fall in love with an ugly beast. Cupid, instead of causing her to fall in love as instructed, took her for himself. He needed the secret to be kept and told her not to look on her husband's face. When she did, he left her. She searched for him everywhere and, as the story unfolded, was subjected to performing menial tasks for Venus.

eɔeɔ

<u>Case Study, Karen</u>:

Karen lived out Psyche's existence. Her husband deserted her. She never understood why but never gave up on him. When he came back at different times, he refused to accept responsibility and would punish her further.

In the classic story, Psyche and Cupid are together in the end. But Karen had to give up looking for the perfect love.

ぐぺぺ

Have you ever found yourself unable to move forward because you refused to let go of a love of your past? If you are still hooked on one, see if you can find Cupid in the background, locate his arrow that has pierced your heart, and pull it out. Begin living for yourself.

Dilemma of Solitary Confinement—Medusa or Midas

Medusa was feared because anyone who looked on her turned to stone. Terror for anyone who approached. The flip side was that she was isolated to herself. Midas provided a similar metaphor. He created incredible wealth for himself but could no longer touch a real person.

Your story might have elements of different myths. One might capture your relationship to your father, and a different one might be relevant to your relationship with your sister. You can begin to understand the themes and see which apply. Knowing the myth can provide a backdrop to understand the archetypal dimensions of the emotional battle you are in. Remember, the old stories do not provide a specific solution. The myths always carry conflict and misdirection. You are required to decide the next steps.

Finding Your Story:

These mythological themes serve a variety of psychological needs. They elicit emotions from us that we didn't realize we had. They explain motivation. They teach you that you can make different decisions than the tragic character of the story. Ultimately, they serve to transform your energy and refocus your goals.

Examine the books you read and the movies you watch. Which trigger your emotions the most? Do you identify with the ordinary person thrust into a drama outside of his or her usual world? Do you find yourself spending time with one-dimensional TV characters that never change and each week suffer the throes of a

Seinfeld-type existence? Do you read horror so that you can at least feel something?

Challenge your conventional beliefs about yourself. Are you like Daniel in the bible, the youngest of the tribe, to be sold off to foreigners as a slave? Does your self-worth exist only when you are able to accomplish the mundane goal set for you by the parent (standing in for the gods)? Does the character in your story show you the way out? Or could you have changed the outcome by making a slightly different choice? Can you see your Achilles heel, be sensitive to it, and not get provoked when someone comes near it? Your story question, like that of all the heroes in literature, is whether you will succeed, be indecisive, or barely survive.

Be careful. When you choose your answer you will be crafting the next chapter in your life story.

CHAPTER 4

EMOTIONAL TRAPS

Recognize the Pattern

You are the writer, director and main character of your life. That doesn't mean that the golden road to success will appear out of thin air. Growth happens through struggle, and resolving conflicts moves you forward. How your personal story follows the patterns of classic mythology shows that your life shares common themes with others. When you see your story against this larger motif, you can face the future with a clearer vision even if it is clouded by emotional turmoil.

Revising Your Story:

At this time, you have probably identified what you want to change in your life. You might be struggling with depression and wondering why the world looks so terrible to you when your friends still enjoy going out. Or your anxiety may be so bad that your comfort zone has shrunk to the four walls of your home. Making sense of your life means rearranging the connections to your story.

Emotionally loaded incidents stick in your memory. Maybe you were left behind by your friends in grade school for what, back then, was a major event. Or you might recall your embarrassment when you were caught shoplifting, cheating on a test, or lying to a friend. The root for the feeling stretches below the surface to connect to the hole in your life, that tragic part of your history you avoid at all costs. Without learning from your past, you're more likely to keep acting out the same old patterns.

Your story includes both the facts of your life and the feelings of your heart. When you're troubled, scribble down your thoughts. This is the best way to capture your immediate reactions and help you identify your feelings. Even if you find only random words coming up, you'll be able to connect them once they appear on paper. Grab a notebook, a loose piece of paper, or a napkin at your local coffee stop. Scatter the emotional terms across the page and see how they flow together. Feelings look completely different written down than they do when they are banging around inside your head.

What you are attempting is more important than just dumping your feelings on the page. To learn about yourself, you need to go beyond what is on your Facebook news feed. While random thoughts might form the initial part of your reflection, linking them together in a meaningful way leads you into a sort of self-analysis. Though you live your feelings every day, committing them to paper makes you the observer as well as owner. A mindfulness develops that allows you to have a personal continuity over time and stay focused on yourself.

Connecting the Dots:

Capture fragments of your emotions as they occur in the moment. Next, link the words by drawing a line between the ones that are related in a meaningful way. This network of lines will reveal how you think about the feeling-toned elements. Intuitively, you will see the relationships and get immediate feedback on your conflicts, your loves, and your hates.

You have to remember that feelings are not cast in concrete, but molded by forms that change shape depending on the situation. Your diagram (sample below) captures a picture of your emotions at the moment. Take that insight and hold that in your heart. Store the notebook or scrap of paper in a folder the same way you would tuck away photos for an album. When you encounter your next conflict or challenge, start with a new page, scratch sheet or napkin. Write down your thoughts, connect the dots, and step back to see the meaning. Keep what has substance, and let go of the rest.

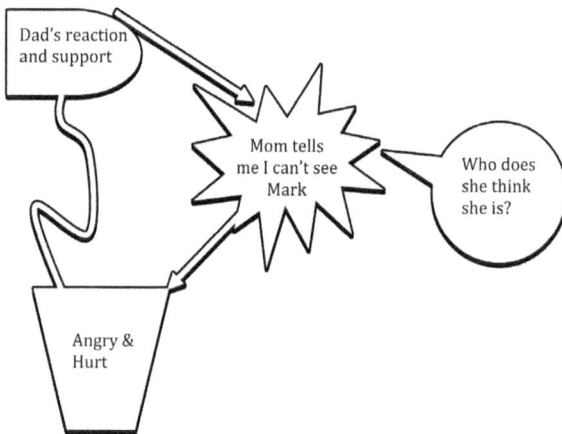

If you get stuck, pull out your folder of old diagrams. Look them over. See which ones resonate. Retain those. Then grab a new page. You'll have thoughts to share, and you'll surprise the observer in yourself.

Gathering Your Soul:

When you can put the feeling element together with your life events, you craft a story that carries an emotional continuity you can touch. You begin to take responsibility for reaching your goals and develop a more complete picture of yourself. Here is where you become the director of the show as well as the main character. Your emotions are not free floating in the stratosphere; they are anchored to experiences that can contribute a sense of chronology to your story.

No doubt you can remember key events in your life without having to write them down. The recording, however, is more of a test of your self-honesty than an aid to memory. The topic of your entries can involve your childhood, your work, or your life as you live it. You record what happened, examine what you want, and outline a plan for change.

Your notes don't just let you look back; they help you look forward. Even if your past contains mistakes, self-destructive behavior, and self-sabotage, you can see the direction of your life and decide to change it. You can heal and choose the path you walk for the rest of the story. You will find meaning in your life, be more comfortable with yourself, and be less susceptible to the denial and avoidance that let you slip into old patterns of dysfunction.

Measuring Progress:

You might have found your own life story in the myths we reviewed in the last chapter. If you did, you have already uncovered some of the negative themes that leave you stuck. You have seen how myths function at the unconscious level and how they convey psychological truths. For example, the parable of the Prodigal Son touches our heartstrings because it tells the universal story of reconciliation. The moral of the story provides guidance that you could apply if you encounter an episode in your life calling for forgiveness. I've never met anyone whose core story doesn't contain a primordial motif. The outline of the pattern is stitched into our nature.

Look for broad themes in your life, and you'll begin to see the fabric of your family story as it intertwines with your own. As you pursue the dialogue through your collection of notes, you will find that the role of your character expands. Your story becomes richer. Having improved vision, you can challenge yourself to enter into that new relationship or to start the new project. Try it out. Write down your feelings. See if it doesn't give you a chance to learn and grow. You can take control of the direction of your life, and nurture yourself the way a good parent would. With love.

Next, meet self-sabotage, your last roadblock to living free. This culprit will invite you to return to the dome.

CHAPTER 5

SELF-SABOTAGE

Defeat the Final Block to Healing

The self-destructive spectrum stretches from stubbing your toe on the piece of furniture you knew was there, to suicide. The middle ground includes the poor health choices people make every day from overeating to smoking. Self-destructive tendencies are the mainstay of dysfunction, and they lead to failed dreams. Oddly enough, self-sabotage will emerge once you reject the insanity of your dysfunctional behaviors. It is then that self-sabotage will step from the shadows, inject doubt into your belief that you can heal, and lead you back to the old familiar habits.

ʘϭʘϭ

Case Study, Nancy:

I'll never forget Nancy, one of my first patients. She had symptoms of depression. The psychiatrist who consulted at the clinic each week thought she suffered from an adjustment disorder, a temporary reaction due to her unwanted pregnancy.

By the fourth session, she showed progress.

"I've decided to keep the baby," she told me.

"Last week, you weren't so sure," I said. "What's changed?"

"It's what Mom and Dad want. Because I live with them, I have to do what they tell me to do. They said they'd help me raise her."

My hope had been that she could feel less victimized, but her choices kept narrowing after she lost her job. The employer told her that her pregnancy had nothing to do with her termination, and yes, she had medical coverage until the end of the month. Her fifth month, thank you very much.

"Has your Dad agreed to help pay to continue your insurance coverage?" I asked.

She nodded and looked at the floor. Even with her head tilted forward and her auburn hair draping her face, I could see the tears trickle down her cheek. She reached for a tissue.

"Will you continue your two courses at the university, then?"

"No. I've withdrawn from the classes and returned the books. I need gas money." She threw the tissue at the trashcan and missed.

"Will you be okay?"

"Yeah."

"Our time is up for today," I said. "Is this an okay place to stop?"

She nodded. Her tears had stopped. She was bracing herself for the return to the cold environment that left her without the lover who fathered the child, the job that had allowed her to escape a verbally abusive home, and the schooling that promised a better life.

"I'll see you next week at this same time," I said.

"Maybe." She started to rise.

A chill shook me from head to foot. "Wait. Sit down."

In prior sessions, she said that crashing her car into a tree would be her plan for suicide. She refused to admit that she intended to head for the large oak, a local landmark, on the way out of town. But when she agreed to a voluntary hospitalization, I knew that she was afraid she might do just that.

In the months following her stay at Memorial Hospital, she lived in her parents' home, gave birth to a healthy baby girl, and recommitted herself to her education. She decided not to live her college days as a single-mom and found adoptive parents through the minister at her family's church. In our last session, she told me, "I'm fine."

Six months later, the picture appeared in the local newspaper of the scarred oak and a crumpled car. Only a caption ran below the photo. Supposedly, the accident that took the life of a 21-year old college student was due to a rain-slick curve. Her mom and dad needed that explanation. But I knew that regardless of the story, regardless of the diagnosis, regardless of the progress that she had already achieved, Nancy had succumbed to the ultimate sabotage.

❧❧❧

Your self-defeating choices need not be as extreme as hers to affect you to the core. No matter how small, they prevent you from moving forward. You stall and desert your goals. Think of when this has happened in your own life. Maybe it was the promise that you'd stick to the exercise plan this time. The first couple of weeks go well, and you start to feel better. Then self-sabotage arrives. The demon voice tells you to skip one session. You cancel the early morning jog after a late night with friends. You missed yesterday's exercise, and you let today's go, too. You have started the slide back to dysfunction. By the third day, you're defeated.

The Slippery Slope of Self-Sabotage:

Just when you think you've changed and escaped dysfunction, self-sabotage appears cloaked as a friend to tell you that you cannot succeed and might as well give up. It plants the seed of fear and then offers you the familiar comfort of your dysfunctional past. Instead of embracing the challenge to move forward, you drift off to consider Christmas of 1993. Self-sabotage gives you an excuse that allows you to dodge accountability. The format is foolproof. "I didn't fail. I caught the flu and didn't have the strength to study."

Are You Slipping?:

How do you know if you are falling into self-sabotage? You have to be alert to the possibility especially in the first thirty days of any change. That window requires the most attention. Within that timeframe, you might encounter any number of self-deceiving sabotages. They tend to fall into certain clusters that you can recognize clearly in retrospect. You have to become sensitive to the signs as they first appear and broaden the options you'd consider.

You will have to call up your courage to face your demon of self-sabotage. Once you do, this adversary will back down, but then it attacks from a different angle. See if any of the following self-sabotages sound familiar. I'll never know which one took Nancy.

Fear of failure: You never seem to make it to the job interview, or you become ill right after achieving the promotion. The physical tendency to get sick is one form of self-sabotage and, as well-known as it is, still often gets accepted as a legitimate excuse.

Threat of the urgent: You have allotted time to a project but then not worked on it at all, letting less important tasks come first. Cleaning your house or taking out the garbage needs to be done but fall into the category of maintenance. If these small jobs constitute the bulk of your activity, you are missing opportunities to grow and further your goals. To overcome this pattern, you have to set the priority level and issue the instructions. Then follow your own orders.

Emotional overload: You tell yourself that you feel alone or too depressed to do anything. The weight of self-pity is burdensome. The problem with self-pity, as with most of these excuses, is that it is dishonest and can easily become a way of life. The Poor Me's are unattractive. They will accompany you to the brink of success and then force you back to square one. They will never stand with you in the winner's circle.

Shame: Shame is buried deep in the core of your being. You feel you don't deserve better. Simple guilt implies a duty to correct a wrong. Shame indicts you of a flaw that can't be washed off. You can't obtain a reprieve from shame.

☙❧❧

Case Studies, Bill, JoEllen, and Mark:

Bill didn't comprehend how he repeatedly failed. He had obtained his M.B.A. and worked for an international firm. When he married and started a family in his hometown, the local newspaper featured him as a rising star. The following month, the district attorney quietly referred him to me for soliciting a prostitute.

The sandy-haired 35-year-old came to the interview in khakis and a dark sweater. "I'll cooperate completely with this evaluation," he said. "I can't believe I did it. It was foolish, but no one got hurt."

"I'm not sure your wife feels that way."

He shifted in his chair. "There's no health risk to her if that's what you mean. I've only done this a couple of times, and it's just been the hand or an occasional blowjob. My physician runs labs whenever I'm worried."

He had fears about the possible consequences, but wanted me to concur with his sense of being caught in a harmless prank. That would be the only way that he could escape the shame of the charge and hide once again under the dome.

"Part of this evaluation is to tell the D.A. if you would benefit from an alternative sentencing program instead of jail," I said.

"You don't have to worry about me," he insisted. "I'm just going to stop."

"Then we have to talk about how you're going to convince me of that."

He turned his hands up in the air. "How do I do that? You must have learned in high school debate that you can't prove the absence of something. I can tell you, however, I am going to stop."

He believed himself. Otherwise, the shame that haunted him would be crushing. In order to preserve his self-esteem, he needed the D.A. to pretend that this never happened. I recommended treatment; the D.A. gave him probation. Even after being shown leniency, Bill's shame destabilized him. I never found out if he re-offended, but he never achieved the success his credentials would have predicted.

Overwhelmed: JoEllen told me that her supervisor assigned increasing numbers of reports to her. Due to her wish to please, she met every deadline, but to do so meant weekends at the office or hauling work home at night. She kept up that pace until a panic attack put her on the side of the road during the drive home one night.

Her regular doctor took her off work for two weeks.

"No one does my job when I'm not there," she said. "It's all going to be stacked on my desk when I get back."

"What will be different this time?" I asked.

"Nothing. They will still expect me to deliver like I did in the past. I'll be snowed under when I walk through the door."

She was her own worst enemy.

"Can you do what you can in the time you have and then go home?"

"No." She let out a sigh. "Just thinking of that makes my chest hurt." She rubbed it with the heel of her hand as if trying to massage a sore muscle.

"Your supervisor's going to have to manage for the couple weeks that you're off."

She blew a puff of air as if extinguishing a candle.

"She called me at home the last two days," she said. "She doesn't know where anything is filed."

"Can you consider just letting her fail?"

She shuddered. "That's just not like me." She stared at me. "That's not how I was raised. I have a strong work ethic."

"The first step," I said, "is to stop taking the calls. She can't fault you when you're not available." This seemed to be sinking in.

By its nature, overwhelm keeps reappearing, and to defeat it you have to refuse to volunteer. When you do, you will shatter the dysfunctional belief that you are indispensible. Then, your value will be built on more than what you produce.

Just not trying: Giving up has to be considered the shortest route for self-sabotage to take you back to dysfunctional attitudes and the acceptance of hopelessness. This is a resignation to the inevitable and an unnecessary surrendering of power. Mark completed his first novel. When the agent who had reviewed fifty pages offered to read the whole manuscript, Mark had lost his "mojo," as he put it, and gave up. For this type, the mantra becomes, "It wouldn't have worked anyway."

ာ

Preventing the Slide—Catching Your Self-Sabotage Early:

The first culprit to restrain is blame. In our culture, when someone is told that he has to make a change, there is the implication that he is doing something wrong. If this is the message you received, you need to correct that. Believing that you are wrong is exactly the type of doubt that self-sabotage nurtures. A no-fault policy is better. That doesn't relieve of your responsibility.

Even my clients, working one-on-one with me, struggle to get free of blame. Being responsible goes beyond the issue of right or wrong. The goal is to be able to talk about the accountability to yourself, without injecting a negative emotional component into the conversation.

You may have fallen back into the junk food habit today. That doesn't mean that you're worthless. See if you can hold the view that you're working to make this plan effective. What matters most is what you do going forward. You learn from mistakes; you do not build on them.

Real accountability is essentially feedback. The blame game uses excuses to shift the focus away from you taking action. The no-fault approach follows the Marine Corps mantra of, "No excuse, sir." You will never drown in shame if you stop, see the wide view, and look for solutions. You are only responsible to yourself. If you're brave enough to stare your excuses in the eye and deny them power over you, you will make better decisions tomorrow.

Solutions:

First, as you move into making a significant life change, mark the next three days on your calendar. During those days, be aware of any excuses you start making for anything. This is a signal that you are on the slippery slope of self-sabotage. Then pause and see if you can claim back responsibility for the events that are happening.

Second, start a Have Done List. This represents a daily priority shortlist and accomplishment record. Record what you do as you do it for that day. Here is where the accountability is tracked. At the end of your day, review the Have Done List. In the right hand margin place a check mark on any of your actions that moved you toward your goal. Place an X in the left hand column for any action that did not.

Re-read the items with the check marks on them. That is what you want to increase. The ones with the X's are most likely maintenance items. Fixing dinner is an excellent example. You have to eat. What else made the list? Maybe grocery shopping, weeding the garden, reviewing the plans for the remodel, or picking up that extra card for the party next week. These maintenance tasks appear efficient in getting things done, but fail to move you toward your goals. Instead, they consume time and let you feel good for having accomplished something. Self-sabotage is allowing yourself to be misdirected.

The Have Done List shows you the places that self-sabotage can creep in. Your assignment is to be aware of what you are doing and to make a conscious choice to push toward your goals. Blaming the weather or the hangover won't work anymore. You might be ill. You could be bedridden. Anything you did that got in your way, you are ultimately responsible for. Yes, even the stubbed toe.

Now that you can take on responsibility for your life, you really can learn to remain in the present and live free.

CHAPTER 6

LIVING FREE

Anchor your new changes
"You can have everything if you let yourself be." –
Anonymous

The plant does not strain in order to grow, and neither should you. You've already recognized the weight of the dome that traps you in dysfunction. You've identified self-destructive tendencies in your past, the fictional myths of your family story, and the lurking menace of self-sabotage. At this stage, you are ready to direct your life in a purposeful way. Organic living is being intimately connected to life and fully present in the moment. You have to stay anchored to keep from losing your direction. Like a ship in a storm, you need a compass to know where true North is. Focus on your goals to stay oriented. Use the three anchors to keep you from drifting back into dysfunction.

Live in the Present Moment:

Change should come naturally. Take a moment. Where are you? At home? At work? On vacation? Breathe in an awareness of the moment, whether it is in the early morning or late at night. Close your eyes. See if you can feel yourself in your body as you occupy this particular location. Watching your breath can help you stay in touch with the moment.

Many people find the mind drifts to memories of the past and worries about the future. This is where dysfunction thrives. The past holds all of your guilt, shame, and regret. The future holds all of your fears. Do you really want to live with those as constant companions?

Stop somewhere in your busy life. You might need to halt the mad dash from project to project, or find a time when the kids are already quiet. Instead of rushing off to the next household duty, take a moment for you. When you find yourself changing tasks, stop. Ask yourself if this is really what you need to commit your time to now. Regardless of what your distraction is, the habit of living in the present takes practice. As with any new skill, you'll get better over time. It will become easier to focus your attention and connect to a sense of serenity.

You don't have to do this alone. Yoga, meditation, journaling, or therapy can give you tools to use. Find a mentor. The right person will help you move forward. Be cautious about the friend, teacher, or even therapist, who only wants to chase away the blues and make you feel better. Remember, you don't have to please them. Don't pretend that everything is okay overnight. Positive change takes time. You will know instinctively whether you are getting more anchored and connected to life, or being recruited to return to hide under the dome.

Living in the moment doesn't alienate you from your past or future. It allows you to develop an awareness of how you set goals and reach them, which leads you to the second anchor.

Observe the Emotional Environment:

Just as you can watch the breath as it goes in and out in a physical sense, you have to pay attention to your feelings. Emotional integration is being able to think about your feelings, as well as have an emotional reaction to your thoughts. The arrow has to go both ways.

Emotional control is achieved when you can observe that process rather than acting on impulse.

The magic of emotional expression is that it exists as a two-person event. You are hard wired neurologically to pick up emotional cues from others. But you can only listen to these cues when you are conscious of your own state. Your receptive circuit can be completely filled with static if your emotional needs drown out any message being sent by the other person.

The achievement of your goals relies on your ability to exercise emotional control. The greatest blueprint is useless in the hands of a fool. If your emotions dominate your planning, your efforts will be disorganized and scattered.

The emotional link to others is crucial to your healing. No one accomplishes all of his/her goals alone. Certain projects can be single-person events, but overall, your success is connected to your ability to work with others. Prove this to yourself. Tomorrow, watch yourself walk through the start of your day. If you are a morning person, that might be when you wake. For some, it might not be until after your first cup of coffee. Whenever you take the personal moment to center yourself on your goals or expectations, observe your emotional temperature. Are you rushed? Irritable? Or just plain tired? Check to see how that feeling carries over to how you talk to others, whether you can listen to them, and ultimately how effective you are in communicating.

The challenge is how you can use this awareness of your emotional state to connect you to life. The act of observing yourself in a non-judgmental way links the emotion, with the thought, with the intention. The next step toward achieving your goal will appear naturally from the integration of these components. You will be centered, see where you are going, and gain a perspective on the importance of the project. Satisfaction wells up not merely from the completion of the project, but from the process of getting there.

Practice this emotional centering with simple tasks, such as brewing coffee or unpacking groceries from the store. When you can quiet yourself and slip into the observing process by focusing on your breathing, you're ready to apply this therapy and alter your life course decisions.

Whether you are chatting with a friend or building a skyscraper, your ability to remain in the moment, fully aware of your emotional state, connects you to your life goals in an organic way. The unconscious is free to cooperate with your conscious plans because it is not fettered to preconceived ideas, old fears, or fantasies of perfection. You can start your planning and action exactly where you are. At this precise moment, you have a supply of all of the resources and strategies for moving forward. Yet for planning to be effective, you still need the third anchor.

Know that Living is a Process:

Life places you on a spiral staircase. You decide whether to walk up or down. Even when you stand still, time is moving forward. You get to choose whether you climb steps to integration or slide down the banisters toward disintegration. You will reach landings that represent plateaus in the healing process. Resting on these enables you to appreciate the growth that has occurred, but you can't stay there for long before you feel the tug to climb higher. This is not about making you feel good, but the search for the next challenge.

The goal is to move forward with an awareness that you are not perfect. If you get stuck on a task, go back to anchor number one and see if you are still moored in the moment. If not, stop, reflect, and look around. Where are you? What is the moment? Re-examine your plans. Do they look any different?

You are now engaged in the process of organic living. Shake free of pre-conceived end points and reassess where you are going. Life is continuous. So are you. There is no buzzer to mark the end of the "first half." Your efforts on your project, no matter what it is, will lead to success, even if you rest on one of the landings. Perfection is for procrastinators who want to put off living. Dysfunctionals live in the glare of the dome, refusing to see where they are or being able to breathe in the moment.

When you live in the moment, even as you march toward a complex goal, the tasks for Tuesday will be different than those for Monday. And not just on a pragmatic basis. Your emotional involvement will be different and clearer if you are viewing it all from the vantage point of this moment.

Are you *here* with me *now*?

Welcome to living free.

About the Author

Dennis Lewis, Ph.D. is a practicing psychologist specializing in the treatment of family dysfunction. For more than twenty-five years, he has been on the clinical faculty of the University of California San Francisco. He serves as a national consultant, expert witness, and media spokesperson. He divides his time between his home in California and the family homestead in Ireland.

www.ingramcontent.com/pod-product-compliance
Lightning Source LLC
Chambersburg PA
CBHW071627040426
42452CB00009B/1527